HOW TO TALK TO ANYONE

OVERCOME DIFFICULT THOUGHTS, SHYNESS, SOCIAL ANXIETY AND LOW SELF-ESTEEM - COMMUNICATE EFFECTIVELY, COMFORTABLY AND CHARISMATICALLY IN ANY SOCIAL SITUATION

WALLACE FOULDS

Text Copyright © 2018 Wallace Foulds

Legal & Disclaimer

The information contained in this book is not designed to replace or take the place of any form of medicine or professional medical advice. The information in this book has been provided for educational and entertainment purposes only.

The information contained in this book has been compiled from sources deemed reliable, and it is accurate to the best of the Author's knowledge; however, the Author cannot guarantee its accuracy and validity and cannot be held liable for any errors or omissions. Changes are periodically made to this book. You must consult your doctor or get professional medical advice before using any of the suggested remedies, techniques, or information in this book.

Upon using the information contained in this book, you agree to hold harmless the Author from and against any damages, costs, and expenses, including any legal fees potentially resulting from the application of any of the information provided by this guide. This disclaimer applies to any damages or injury caused by the use and application, whether directly or indirectly, of any advice or information presented, whether for breach of contract, tort, negligence, personal injury, criminal intent, or under any other cause of action.

You agree to accept all risks of using the information presented inside this book. You need to consult a professional medical practitioner in order to ensure you are both able and healthy enough to participate in this program.

Table of Contents

INTRODUCTION

For most people, talking is as important as breathing. Verbalizing our thoughts and feelings with other human beings is so central for our survival, that even in our attempts not to communicate, we still "say" something. Try to stay silent for a few days— you will feel like stuck inside your own body. Even the newborns need to communicate from the moment they're born to maintain their survival. Our communication efforts form our self-identity and our behavior is adopted and adapted in response to the messages we transmit and receive from others.

The desire to talk is hardwired into all of us. Even before the development of language, our ancestors used to share information about food supplies, dangerous animals, and weather patterns with fellow humans. They also knew what behavior is appropriate and how to act in certain situations. Our livelihood, the satisfaction of our basic needs and ultimately, our existence depends upon mastery of an intricate set of communication rules and behaviors.

Although we all communicate, the ability to do it proficiently and with purpose is something we develop with knowledge, practice and experience. Good communication is about the way we give our thoughts a voice and listen what others has to say.

We are social creatures and hugely dependent on our ability to talk to make our way through the world. But for some people, social interaction and talking to people becomes an anxiety filled experience. Many people don't feel comfortable speaking at all in any sort of public situation. But speaking anywhere with confidence can improve every aspect of your life— it can get you the best jobs, more respect and authority in workplace, finest spouses and greatest friends. It can make you a leader among your peers. Your ability to speak effectively with people can work as the stepping-stones to success in your personal and professional life. This book is here to explain the audiences how to overcome the fear of conversation and talk to anyone with confidence.

CHAPTER 1

The Value of Conversation

With the advancement of technology we are more connected than ever before. We can now use various types of communication mediums such as telephone and email. But our conventional wisdom tells us that the greatest result is achieved in face-to-face verbal communication. The art of oral communication like any other art is a skill of elegance, nuance and creative execution. Learning the art of oral communication or attaining the conversation mastery will get us more from life.

We all came across individuals who can talk to anyone about anything with effortless ease. And while it is true that there are people who are born with this gift, luckily for the rest of us the expertise in conversation can be developed and mastered.

Conversation is a spontaneous form of communication—which is usually less formal and more flexible. As it is interpersonal, there is a high level of understanding and transparency in this form of communication. We enter conversations for purposes of pleasant engagement in order to discuss new ideas, revisit old ones and spark a bit of lively discussion. Conversation will come into play when we meet new people and enjoy social interactions.

Conversation solves life's problems: conflicts, disputes and many issues/differences can be put to an end by talking them over. If you want to promote a receptive and encouraging morale among the employees of your company, you'll need to develop conversational skill.

Your conversational skill will help you get promoted. You may have all the technical expertise and experience to deserve the next promotion, but if you don't have the required conversational skill to back it up, you might miss the chance to level up in your career. Lack of communication will make your efforts less visible to the people who can land that promotion.

With the help of conversational mastery, you will be able to communicate everything that will contribute for your career growth. Your charismatic speaking ability will not only give you a good edge compared to your peers, but it will also help you to earn the general goodwill of most people in your company. People will naturally like you and establish you as someone who is trustworthy and a great person to work with if you are gracious with your words as you are outstanding in your performance. Skillful conversation eases the gaps that arise between individuals who have very little or almost nothing in common.

Barriers to Communication

We already know the importance of oral communication. Good communication has undoubtedly contributed to the unprecedented quality of life many of us enjoy. Poor communication on the other hand, contributes to the social isolation, deprivation and much of the misery of modern life. You may wonder if oral communication is so necessary, what stops us from being eloquent in conversation. Why many people struggle to articulate themselves?

The following hindrances prevent us from being good communicators. If you can overcome these barriers, you can literally mold yourself into a great communicator and a brilliant conversationalist.

Social anxiety

During effective communication, you use several areas of your brain at the same time. One area may manage your listening ability, another part may make sense of what the other person is saying, while another part may formulate what to respond with. These processes take lots of concentration, and if a brain is overwhelmed with anxious thoughts, the communication becomes quite difficult. Anxiety in any form impairs communication, and the fear of talking tends to present in every form of anxiety. Fear of talking is most commonly associated with social phobia or social anxiety disorder.

People with social anxiety feel fear of being scrutinized or judged by others in any social interaction. Their fear makes them to avoid situations that cause anxiety. The signs of social anxiety may include fear of situations in which you may be judged, fear of being embarrassed or humiliated, fear of interacting or talking with strangers, avoiding speaking to people out of fear of embarrassment and expecting the worst possible consequences from negative experience during a social event. People with social phobia avoid interacting unfamiliar people or strangers, starting conversations and attending parties or social gatherings. They make very poor eye contact during conversation and have a very low self-esteem.

When you have social anxiety, you may worry that you will say something wrong and embarrass yourself. You might also feel tensed anticipating that people expect you to be more charming and witty than you know you actually are. Although intrinsically you know that most of your fears are irrational, you can't get rid of them despite your best effort. The most common subset of social anxiety is glossophobia or the fear of public speaking, which affects 3 out of 4 people. That means 75% people suffer from speech anxiety. According to a study, the fear of public speaking is more common fear than any other fear including the fear of death.

Dealing With Fear of Talking

There are various techniques to conquer the fear of talking. The best technique is to meet it head-on. If you feel scared of embarrassing yourself in conversation, the next time you are in a social event, take a deep breath and walk up to someone who is not currently talking to anyone and introduce yourself with a smile. The social situation itself does not generate much anxiety, large part of the fear stems from the thoughts of what could potentially happen. If you walk over and say, "Hi I think I've seen you around, but we haven't officially met. My name is David", then you're eliminating the possibility that the other person is going to come over and put you on the spot. Moreover, when you start the conversation you can control the conversation's directions. So why feel scared about what to say when someone walks up to you, introduces herself and sets the topic of conversation? You will appear more relaxed and confident if you are in control of the conversation— that happens when you say hello first.

The fear of rejection may also stop you from getting acquainted with new people in a social event. You may go over to someone who looks interesting enough, and when you are in the middle of the conversation, that person politely excuses himself and goes over to talk to his friends. You may also find that he enjoys their company lot more than he was enjoying yours. In this case it is quite normal to feel rejected, which can be hard on your ego. If you are naturally introvert or shy, a rejection can be your worst nightmare.

People with social anxiety believe they are uninteresting, boring and not good enough. A rejection reinforces these negative beliefs and crushes their self-esteem. They start to feel that they're not worth talking to and nobody wants to be around them.

If rejection makes you feel miserable, know that rejection is a common experience even among those who go on to be tremendously successful. If a person leaves the talk after a short, superficial conversation may be not because you're uninteresting or unattractive— it may because he does not really know you. It is quite normal that some people you will meet along the way will reject you and not want to talk. This happens to everyone no matter how interesting they are. Don't let rejection to get you down. The best way to make that rejection seem less significant is to meet more people and make more attempts at conversation.

We all get rejected. The sooner you accept the rejection and move on with your life, the easier a time you're going to have. Don't take rejection as personal attacks— don't allow it to flatten you. It is important to get over the fear of rejection because feeling fearful will keep you stuck in low confidence, which will significantly lower your likelihood of success in making friends.

Self-Disclosure

Self-disclosure means that you are going to reveal information about yourself to another person and allow them to know you. People are interested to know about the person they are communicating with. If your process of self-disclosure gives a negative impression, they will tend to avoid you. In an ideal self-disclosure process, the information should be shared from both sides. If you overwhelm your counterpart with too much information about yourself or information they really have no interest in, you'll lose their interest— because you are appearing as self-centered and selfish. The concept is simple— when you are disclosing yourself, you are letting people know who you are, and it's easier for people to relate to you as a real human being with goodness and imperfections... with thoughts and emotions. When you are perceived as a human (not someone easily depersonalized), the communication will be more effective and the relationship will improve.

Self-disclosure does not have to be profound or meaningful in the first meeting. Superficial self-disclosure, usually in the form of "small talk" is a powerful strategy to initiate a relationship.

When you are addressing to a group (public speaking), it is always better to break the depersonalization barrier by sharing some information about yourself in the beginning of your speech. One of the best ways to self-disclosure in groups is to share a personal story that is relevant to reason why the group is meeting.

Not everyone is equally transparent and willing to self-disclose. Some can naturally reveal their personal information, others can hesitate to disclose information mainly because of fear of rejection and/or loss of privacy. Deciding when to disclose something in a conversation is equally as important as deciding whether or not to disclose at all. Disclosing information at a wrong time in a conversation can produce negative results. Therefore it is important to consider whether to disclose information early, in the middle or late in the conversation. Sometimes it is wise to wait until the middle of the conversation, as you have some time to understand the other person's mood and set up the tone for your disclosure. As self-disclosure involves some personal risks, it is important to decide how much information you should share. If the person you are conversing with is known to be loose-lipped with other person's information, then you should be very careful in choosing what to share with them.

Self-disclosures can be unplanned. You can be in situation where someone is asking you a direct personal question and you don't have enough time to think through any potential risks before disclosing information. In this case, if you don't feel comfortable answering, you can choose to give an indirect or general answer.

Remember self-disclosure is irreversible. You can't un-disclose something you've just disclosed. Nor you can control how people perceive you on the basis of your disclosure. In cross-cultural communication it is important to examine the rewards and risks of self-disclosure in terms of particular cultural rules.

Conversation Killer Attitudes

Negative attitudes are the conversation killers. Some of these attitudes may stem from fear; some can come from misconception and some are the just the result of bitterness and envy.

One of the common attitudes that ruin the conversation is the thought that a conversation has to be an argument. People with this attitude first determines how their point of view differs from that of their counterparts', then pick it apart in favor of their own "superior" point of view. They always tend to "prove" their counterpart is wrong, no matter how rational they sound. If the arguer is not especially tactful, he may say, "Well, I think that's a stupid idea" or "who told you such thing?" or "do you really believe that"? They are almost always on the defensive side and their mantra is "I object".

People who are always argumentative are usually afraid of being wrong. Losing an argument make them feel vulnerable and helpless. The more arguments they win, the more they believe their arguments as being right. It becomes really hard to get them to consider other person's views because in their mind, they are always right. Some of the argumentative people display strong narcissistic tendencies, which can be annoying to their colleges. People with argumentative attitude usually have a very little or no idea about how their behaviors impact others. They think that they appear more intelligent than their counterpart, but in reality they come off more like bullies.

Now, how can you know that you are being argumentative? Next time you are talking to somebody, observe your response when your partner says something with which you disagree. Do you feel a strong urge to tell them that they are wrong? Do you automatically jump to "correct them"? If the answer is "yes", then you have got argumentative attitude.

The Right Way to State Your Position

In order to change the argumentative mentality, first we have to understand that anyone can be wrong, and we are also probably wrong about lots of things. If someone's holds a different point of view, instead of immediately disproving it, we have to understand why he has that opinion. We can ask question and show a genuine interest to understand. This will not just encourage more conversation, but also encourage your partner to open up to again.

Explore the deeper meaning behind your argumentative attitude. May be you lack the sense of self-worth and seek to gain it through arguments.

If you want to disagree with someone and state your opinion without ruining the conversation, here are the guidelines you have to follow:

1. When you are prioritizing logic over emotion, you're disagreeing respectfully. If you feel that the views of your partner don't seem logical, avoid making statements that put her ideas down. Statements such as, "it is a stupid idea", or "how could you possibly think that?" may negatively impact the discussion. That person may feel offended and insult your idea, the same way you insulted hers. As a result you conversation may turn into a yelling match. You will have much better chance to get your point across, if you avoid making derogatory remarks or using sarcasms.

2. Wait until your partner is done expressing her opinion then calmly state your argument. You can start by saying, "well, I think..." or "I'm afraid I disagree" or "I have a completely different opinion on that".

3. Remain calm and make sure to state all the points of your arguments. While you're stating your arguments, your partner may try to debate you on a particular point. In this case politely remind her that you listened

to her points and you will appreciate her doing the same.

4. Once you're done, allow the other person express his or her views. Don't interrupt— patiently listen her points before you respond. In an argument people often get emotional about the subject, and tend to interrupt frequently. Keeping the emotions away can help you to enjoy a great discussion.

5. If your counterpart gets impatient or angry, let her know that she will have their chance to speak after you have had your say. And when your partner is having her turn, make sure not to interrupt; otherwise you come up as hypocritical.

6. After continuing the argument for a while, if you discover that it is not possible to find any common ground with your partner, it is wise to gracefully withdraw. Remember, the other person has the right to her views, even though you know she is wrong. Let her know that although you disagree with her opinion, you respect it.

Asking For Clarification

If you are afraid to admit that you have no idea what your partner is talking about, the conversation will be halted. Sometimes when the topic of discussion is shifted, some people tend to display that they have a good understanding on the new topic, on which they have no knowledge at all. With a very little knowledge, you might still be able to bluff your way through the conversation, but since you are failing to add anything meaningful to the discussion, the conversation will be a boring experience for both of you. Moreover, if your counterpart senses that you are lying, he will lose interest in the discussion. Instead of faking, it is wise to admit that you have no knowledge on the topic and ask your partner to explain it. Your partner will feel encouraged to share his knowledge with you. You will also feel good as you are learning something new. The conversation will be an enjoyable experience— all it costs is some false ego.

Breaking the Stereotype

Our brain is hardwired to make quick response— it tends to make a snap judgment about somebody or something based on the immediately visible characteristics. This is apparently harmless, but when people start those stereotypes beyond immediate impulse, it can lead to things such as prejudice, discrimination and sadly bullying. Stereotyping is a major barrier to communication. When the stereotypes are believed as true, it's called "bias".

When we stereotype, we make judgments about people based on their appearance, color, clothing or hairstyle. For instance, seeing a man covered in tattoos, one may think that he is arrogant or he owns a motorcycle— but that does not mean that it is true.

As stereotyping discourages communication, and does not allow us to know a person from scratch, when you find yourself stereotyping someone, you have to find out whether your assumptions are true. Ask questions about him, particularly about the part you think you already know. Avoid making comments about him based on your stereotypes.

Dealing With Attention Craving

We all have the natural feeling of wanting to connect and be acknowledged by others. Being acknowledged by others, and knowing that people value your views is a huge boost to your confidence. While desiring attention at times is completely human, some people wants all eyes on them at all times and are not happy until the entire conversation is about them and on the areas they are interested in. Some attention seekers like to always brag to others about their accomplishment and talents in a hope of being recognized for excellence. There are other types of attention seekers, whose behavior derived from others pitying them. This type of individuals may whine or complain incessantly about their life and failures ("no one likes me", "I'm a stupid", "I'm born unlucky", "I wish I die"). Nevertheless, their intention is to gain attention and also reassurance. There are various kinds of attention seekers and they are known by many names (spotlight hogs, drama queens), but their actions are the same.

Sociologist Charles Derber performed a research on face-to-face interactions. After analyzing 1500 conversations he found that despite good intentions, and often unconsciously, most people struggle with what he termed as "conversational narcissism".

We all want to share our ideas in a conversation. But we have to remember that a conversation should not be a solely individual endeavor— it has to be a group effort. An ideal conversation is like a song where the rhythm is a critical element; and each member of the group must contribute to keep the rhythm going. If you constantly demand all the attention in conversation, people will lose interest and fewer people will want to talk to you.

But how do you know that you are struggling with conversational narcissism? Next time when you have a conversation with someone, be aware of your feeling. Do you feel the craving for turning the attention back to yourself shortly after your counterpart starts talking? Do you tend to dominate the conversation from that point on? Do you tend to ask questions that shift the topic of conversation towards you? If the answer of those questions is "yes", then you have to understand that to make conversation a good experience, each of the participants has to sacrifice a little to increase the pleasure each individual receives. Your counterpart also deserves to get some attention.

Some people tend to adopt subtler ways to hog the spotlight. They steal the conversation while appearing to be a part of the conversation in progress. Here is an example: somebody is telling a story about a new car he just bought. Upon listening, the attention seeker says, "you know that reminds me of the deal I got on my new sports car", and the conversation is shifted towards him. Responses can take two forms, "shift-response" and "support-response". The previous conversation was an example of "shift-response". Here is the example of support-response:

Bob: I'm thinking about buying a new car

Steven: Oh really? What models have you looked at?

In order to get rid of "conversational narcissism" we have to adopt support-response, instead of shift-response. Healthy conversations should be co-operative, not competitive. But many people unknowingly turn conversations into competitions. When you find yourself in a conversation, where you're more knowledgeable on the subject than your counterparts, take a while to judge the level of discourse and try to match it. You can also ask supportive questions like, "Why did you feel that way?"

Support-question is paramount in a conversation, because when the support-response is withdrawn it can kill someone's story dead on tracks especially by not asking any questions. You might be asking whether there is any time you should be getting all the attention in a conversation. The answer is yes. If someone asks your expert opinion on something, you can hog the spotlight for a few minutes. For instance, if you are an engineer, and someone asks your opinion about a specific engineering project, you can talk for a couple of minutes. If you are looking for an arbitrary guideline of when it's time to stop talking, try talking for a couple of minutes. Then pause, and see if the audience wants to hear more about that topic. If they seem to still be interested you may continue for a little longer. Occasionally you might want to pause to see if anyone has questions. When they ask questions, listen patiently. Find a balance between listening and talking.

Remember all conversations are not discussion. People often use conversation as a way to keep the good mood going. Therefore you don't have to argue and have to be right about every topic. If you "win" every conversation, nobody will enjoy that. Instead sit back, relax and keep the rhythm going.

Self-esteem

If you find it hard to believe that you are someone people would love to talk to and that prevents you from initiating a conversation; or, if you think starting a conversation will make other people offended; or if you think yourself a boring person that no one wants to talk to, then you will probably need to improve your self-esteem.

People with low self-esteem lacks confidence in themselves. They are afraid that they will not succeed. They question whether they can keep what they have managed to attain. They fear that if they reveal themselves, people will think less of them. They are in constant fear of losing things that are valuable to them, such as job, money and relationships.

Low self-esteem is a strong barrier to communication that affects many areas of an individual's life. People with low self-esteem sometimes develop fear of social situations, what makes their everyday relationships with friends and social events a nightmare. Their fear of failure in social situations makes them avoid parties and other social gatherings. They tend to be pessimistic towards people and groups within society. Low self-esteem makes people downplay their accomplishments. They berate themselves for their mistakes than they praise themselves for their triumphs. They develop a sense of worthlessness and often interpret critical feedback, romantic rejections or unsuccessful job applications as evidence to support their views. Fortunately there are tons of resources available to help you boost your self-esteem and make you feel good about who you are.

Improving Your Self-Esteem

Best place to begin is with your thoughts. Psychologist Eugene Sagan used the term "the pathological critic" to describe negative inner voice that attacks and judges people. Inner voice is present in everyone. But if one's self-esteem is low, his pathological critic or inner voice can be more vicious and vocal. If anything goes wrong, the critic starts to blame that person. This is the force within the mind that compares you with others and makes you feel down. It sets impossible standards of perfection and beats you up for the smallest mistakes. Pathological critic discourages you to meet someone and start a conversation. This critic tries to make you believe that you are stupid, incompetent and weak. This voice is so insidious, that most people fail to notice its devastating effect.

In order to gain control of this critic, first you have to hear him. You'll need especial vigilance to catch the critic in the act of putting you down. Notice when the critic make comments like, "you're bad at conversation" or "you're weak". The critic is louder in problematic situations such as when you meet strangers, converse with people you find sexually attractive, interact with authority figures or situations in which you've made a mistake and feel criticized and defensive. Monitor your critic in problematic situations and write down the negative self-talks. The more of those self-talks you list, the better. Pat yourself on the back if you can catch at least ten critic's barbs each day.

At night, get a piece of paper and draw a line down the middle. On the left side, put the heading, "Helps me avoid feeling" and the right side put the heading, "Helps me feel or do". Now for each critic's barb you listed in the notebook, write down the function of that thought— how it motivated you do something or avoid feeling something unpleasant.

Here are some examples:

Thought number	Helps me to feel or do	Helps me to avoid feeling
01	Motivated to put attention to details	
02		Being judged in front of my colleagues.

As you do this exercise, you'll discover that some of the critic's attacks made you feel awful; but some of the attacks drove you to higher level of achievement and self-improvement. As you are equipped with the new knowledge now, you are ready for the most important stage, "disarming the critic".

Here are the steps to disarm the critic:

Step one: Unmasking the purpose

Step two: talking back

Unmasking the critic involves exposing the critic's true purpose. Sit down, take a few deep breaths and relax. Now think what is the true purpose of the critic.

Here are some examples of ways you might unmask him.

- You're telling me that she hates me so that I won't feel hurt if she rejects me.

- You're saying it's impossible for me so that I won't bother trying and won't have to be worried about messing everything up.

- You're pushing me to become perfect so that I work harder to become the best version of myself.

As you now know the critic's ulterior motive, you'll feel less intimidated by his rants and raves, and take his comments less seriously. Now you're going to undermine his message by talking back.

In the second step, you'll refute and reject the critic's message. There are various ways to do that. One of the ways is using a psychological cannon to blow the critic away so that he finally shuts up. The Howitzer Mantras are designed to hit the critic like cannon blasts. Here are some of them:

- Get off my back!

- Stop you liar!

- Shut up!

- Stop this shit!

- This is poison. Stop it!

The point of uttering these mantras is to feel angry. Shout these mantras in your mind. It is perfectly healthy to use these profanities against the critic. Another way to disarm the critic is to use positive affirmations. Here are some of them:

- I am sound in body mind and spirit

- I have all it takes

- I am superior to negative thoughts

- I am in charge of my mind

- I am fearless

- I am a powerhouse

- I am indestructible

- I am resilient

- I am a silent warrior

- I am patient and tolerant

- I let go of the sorrow and embrace the bliss

- I am at peace with all that has happened, is happening and will happen.

- I forgive myself and set myself free

- I love and accept of myself.

- I love my life

- I am loving and loveable

- I am kind and caring

- I radiate beauty, charm and grace

- I find joy and pleasure in most simple things in life

- I choose to be happy

- All is well in my world

Improving your self-esteem is a process. It will take a while to get rid of the negativities you believed for ages. Therefore be patient and stick to your practice.

CHAPTER 2

The Art of Socializing

Social skill is one of the most critical sets of abilities we can have. Socializing and connecting with others is a fundamental human need. When this need is not met, we feel depressed and lonely. So how do you feel about your social skill?

In order to socialize effectively it is important to know your strengths and weaknesses in areas like conversation style, attitude, physical presence, personal revelation and response to others. Ask yourself the following questions:

Conversation style: Do you enjoy long conversation or prefer limited talk time?

Attitude: Do you try to appear as a positive individual or do you bring whatever you are feeling to the social occasion with you? Are you confident about your social abilities?

Physical presence: How do you generally feel about your appearance? Do you think a change in hairstyle or wardrobe boost will put you in the right mood for socializing?

Personal revelation: How comfortable do you feel talking about yourself? Some people can easily reveal personal information, others are very careful about revealing themselves. Do you comfortably talk about your skills and expertise?

Response: What is the nature of your response to others? Do you think that you are perceived as friendly, kindhearted, and supportive?

Reviewing these essential personality areas can improve our ability to intuit how people see us, and this helps us to authentically connect with other humans, and obtain deep satisfaction that comes with those ties. Often we negatively judge our personality type and think of it as unchangeable. But every one of us is brilliantly multilayered. We can choose which aspect of our personality we would bring out at any given time.

Examining your traits can be insightful for you. Understanding your strengths and weaknesses is not for the purpose of self-judgment. Having this knowledge will help you to focus on the particular steps, which will bring desired result from social interactions.

What is Your Personality Type?

One of the subtle obstacles that stand in the way of creating rapport is the clash of different personality types. If you happen to be a person who considers all the practical aspects of a problem before making a decision, and you have a communication with someone who depends on his gut feeling to make choices, the chances of you and his being able to effectively communicate is very slim. In order to hold meaningful conversations with different personality types, you need to have some understanding on how different personality types communicate.

Psychological theorist Isabel Briggs Myers and her mother Katharine Cook Briggs developed an inventory of personality types based on the conceptual theories proposed by Carl Jung. Myers-Briggs Type Indicator (MBTI) is a commonly accepted way to find out your personality type. MBTI grades your personality by asking you questions. MBTI questionnaire can be easily found online. Based on your answers, you will fall into one side or another of four major dichotomies.

The four pairs of main dichotomies are: Introversion & extroversion, thinking & feeling, sensing & intuitive, Judgment & perception. These four pairs of dichotomies combine to form your personality type. Every personality type has their unique way of communication, which other personality type may not understand. However there are guidelines for communicating with each dichotomy type:

Introverts: These types of individuals are comfortable doing things alone. They know how to enjoy the solitude. Introverts are not spontaneous conversationalists— they often feel intimidated, bored or exhausted by social interactions. But they are naturally good at understanding non-verbal communication. Because of their reserved natures, they are not interested to form wide network of friends and acquaintances— they rather prefer a small group of close friends. Getting to know an introvert is not easy; but when you get to know them, you'll be amazed to find out how excellent they are as a conversation partner.

Unfortunately the introverts seem less visible when placed next to extroverts. Introverts are often misunderstood and even underestimated because of their quietness. Extroverts may view introverts as antisocial or types of people who don't want other's company.

While interacting with an introvert, we have to respect their privacy. You may have to resist the urge to carry on the conversation with them, unless they show inclination for discussion. Instead, allow them to speak, and become an active listener. Introverts take time to open up— therefore you have to be patient. If you are an extrovert, you may sometime find these personality types quite boring. But you have to remember that they have different brain chemistry, different thought process than you. In time when you get to know them, you'll be staggered to learn how good they are in conversation.

Extroverts: Extroverts appear bright; they seem more talkative and generally show warm interest in their surroundings. They are easy to talk to. They are prone to action than contemplation and they enthusiastically participate in group activities. They are outspoken and feel free to share their personal information. An extrovert would prefer talking to you in person rather than over telephone or through e-mail.

Although extroverts are good at initiating small talk, they are not perfect at holding conversation with others. Sometimes they don't think before they speak, which may hurt other's feelings. They dominate the conversation when talking to introverts. Introverts may not enjoy their talkativeness. They may also see them as insincere.

As you interact with an extrovert, you have to keep in mind that extroverts have a natural expertise in small talks. To keep the conversation going, you have to make sure that you appear interesting while taking to them, and give constant feedback about how you feel.

Feelers: Feelers are naturally friendly and empathetic to others. They are more respectful to other people's values. As they are more concerned with emotions, they understand other's emotions better than the other personality types. Their emotion motivates them to perform better in their professional life.

While interacting with feelers, make sure that your ideas are meaningful to them in some way. Don't forget to praise them for their achievements.

Thinkers: These personality types prefer logic and objective analysis. They look for the most correct answers. These types of individuals are very precise and fair-minded in their style of thought. They enjoy discussions and debates.

While interacting with a thinker, you have to focus on the facts. Keep small talks to minimum. Thinker will enjoy conversing with you if you can analyze the fact and point out the pros and cons.

Sensors: People of this personality are very detail oriented. They are concerned with logic; therefore you will need to take logical approach while conversing with a sensor. This type of individuals can be pessimistic. They are good at problem solving and always look for problems to solve. Timeliness is one of their top priorities.

While conversing with a sensor, it is better to avoid using metaphors. These types of individuals are usually not convinced by emotion or enthusiasms. Therefore discuss things that are already possible, and draw logical conclusions based on the factual information.

Intuitives: Intuitives depend on their gut feeling to make decisions. They are opposite to sensors. They tend to rely on their imaginations rather than facts. They use the right hemisphere— area of the brain that controls emotions. Other personality types often find it difficult to understand their ideas. Intuitives frequently use metaphors and symbols, which the sensors and thinkers may find annoying. Practical minded people may find conversing with intuitives as waste of time.

While interacting with this personality type, make sure to express your opinions in an original way. You are free to use symbols and metaphors.

Judgers: Judgers are goal-oriented. They like to plan their work and work their plan. They tend to show little restraint when it comes to expressing their views, feelings and preferences. A wise judger tends to collect as much information as possible before drawing a conclusion. They are generally inflexible and don't like surprises. They are very organized.

While communicating with judges, you have to be decisive. Judgers like timeliness, so you might want to be timely as you communicate with this personality type.

Perceivers: Perceivers believe that there can be multiple ways to approach something. They are flexible in their thinking. Perceivers are open to new ideas— they can accommodate different point of views. They usually take longer to respond to a situation, as they try to understand its complexity. Unlike judgers, perceivers love surprises. One of their key strengths is that they always tend to look for new information and opportunities. They show surprising amount of interest in different fields of work. As they have no fixed plan, they can experiment with new ideas and can easily change directions.

While communicating with perceivers, you can talk about new ideas and possibilities.

In the next chapter we will learn how to interact with people using positive body language

CHAPTER 3

The Role of Body Language

When we interact with other human beings, we broadcast information in various ways. Some information is verbalized, the rest are embodied. The process of communication not only involves exchange of words, but exchange of gestures. And the recognition and appropriate response to physical gestures greatly influence the outcome of a communication. A small positive gesture can worth a thousand words. Misusing body language whether accidentally or deliberately, can negatively affect the conversation, even before the words are exchanged. Some people wonder why no one wants to talk to them; it may be because their body language that inadvertently tells others to keep the distance.

Sometimes you only have seconds to get someone's attention before initiating a conversation. In those few seconds you have to form a good impression by communicating with your counterpart non-verbally. And just by looking at your body language, your counterpart will decide immediately if you're approachable for conversation or if you would rather be left alone. Learning to understand the non-verbal cues is like upgrading our current system of communication.

Not knowing the true meaning of physical gestures may cause us to misread a signal. As non-verbal behavior is complex and subtle, it can be frequently misinterpreted. For instance, employees often feel neglected and irritated when the bosses don't make eye contact when they speak. Some bosses tend to get busy with other works when an employee is addressing them. They check their emails, shuffle papers, check their watch, check out the room... they look at anywhere but the speaker. In this case, may be the employer doesn't mean to disrespect the employee, but the employee interprets his body language as the signs of negligence.

Several studies have been performed on body language. One of the studies performed by Hickson, Stacks and Moore in 2004, revealed that during conversation, people transmit between 63 and 93 percent of the information nonverbally. Therefore learning how to read other's body language and knowing how to use your body language is paramount for being a good communicator. While most of the non-verbal information is transmitted unconsciously, the good news is, you can intentionally use the non-verbal hints to appear friendly, sociable and attractive. Just as the good selection of clothing makes the best impression in interview, employing the right body language will attract people towards you and make you popular among your friends and peers.

Guideline For Using Good Body Language

Positive body language makes people more receptive to the idea of going up and talking to you. When you deliver positive non-verbal hints, you appear open, inviting and sociable. Body language is not something that has to be mastered, like sign language. We all have been using body language from the moment we were born. For example the newborns exhibit a handful of physical gestures when they feel happy or uncomfortable. When you scowl at the cup you're holding, you're non-verbally saying that you're not enjoying the coffee.

Therefore to create a good impression, all you have to do is to be aware of the bodily hints that invite communication. Here are some common gestures of non-verbal communication:

- Smiling

- Making appropriate eye contact

- Keeping the arms open and inviting

- Establishing physical contact where applicable (i.e. shaking hands)

- Nodding occasionally

- Leaning forward to display your interest while someone is talking.

Making the world smile with you:

Smile reflects the positive attitude, friendliness, openness and sends out non verbal invitation for other people to smile back. It is important to smile as you meet someone.

But how should you smile at someone? According to conversational expert Leil Lowndes, "when see someone don't immediately break out into a smile. Instead stare at the person for a second. Take their measure, as your grandparents might have said. Then let a smile spread across your face".

When someone smiles from the heart, their lips get separated revealing the upper and lower teeth. The smile envelops the face and wrinkles appear at the edges and below the eyes. True smile is contagious and transmits to the faces of the listeners. But when the smile is fake or meant for courtesy, lips remain tight and stretched horizontally. Cheeks lift slightly up and the teeth remain behind the closed lips. Although people sometimes intentionally hide their teeth during smiling, a genuine smile brightens the eyes and accompanies other facial features, which don't go unnoticed.

Remember to keep your chin up as you smile. Keeping the chin up not just broadcasts your smile to rest of the crowd, but it also makes you appear receptive and confident. Notice the how charismatic communicators smile in the social gatherings— you will see their chins are up, broadcasting their smile to the rest of the world.

Welcoming with open arms:

When your arms are open, you are displaying openness— this signal shows that you are approachable. You may feel comfortable with your arms crossed, but it is a defensive and gesture that may discourage your counterpart to continue the conversation. Therefore avoid crossing your arms and legs during friendly interaction.

Proximity is also important here. Personal space varies among males and females, also among cultures. If you are meeting people for the first time, moving too close can make them uncomfortable, and standing too far can also give wrong message. However the ideal personal space between friends (not intimate couples) is 3 feet.

Stand in a comfortable position, drop you're your arms by your sides. Don't slouch. If you are sitting, you can lean forward during the conversation to show you are interested in what the speaker has to say.

For some people the habit of arm crossing can be very strong. To overcome this habit, you can keep your one hand occupied by holding a drink and carry it around. Women have an advantage here if they use small purse, which they can use to keep the hands occupied and prevent them from crossing.

If you don't feel comfortable with holding a glass all the time, here are few other techniques to keep your arms uncrossed:

- Sticking the hands in your pants pocket

- Hitching your thumbs to your belt loops

- Draping your jacket over one arm.

If you keep your hands busy during a conversation, you can apply another technique of a positive body language "touching". Touch can convey the emotional messages. There is a subject called 'Haptics', in the body language spectrum, which studies the signals transmitted by human touch. Handshake is a great way to get acquainted and initiate a conversation. When you meet someone, stick out your hand

and offer it for the other person to shake. In the business world, handshake is the most powerful bonding tool.

Touch is also a great way to inspire your team members. Touch can be complimentary; it can also be an expression of sympathy; either way it can create a bond between the team members. But we have to be careful about choosing the right event where the touching is applicable.

Studies suggest that hand gestures have a close link with speech and with social perception and persuasion processes. We should remember that hand gestures are not just random hand flapping; we have to ensure that the movements of our hands are relevant to the words we speak.

In order for successful communication, we have to adopt positive gestures to win people over. Our postures not just affect other's perception about ourselves, they also affect our mood, therefore we can deliberately change our postures to feel positive and demonstrate positive expressions.

Showing Your Interest:

During a face-to-face conversation, it is important to pay attention to your body language to let your counterpart know that you are interested in what she has to say. If you're in a sitting posture, lean slightly forward to show your partner that you're interested in what she is saying. During long conversations, some people like to lean back to feel relaxed while listening; but this can give their counterpart the message that they are not taking it seriously. Avoid leaning too much; this may make your partner uncomfortable.

Making Eye Contact:

Eyes are the most important transmitter of your emotions and motives. Smile and make eye contact during the introduction. In an ideal conversation, the speaker makes eye contact 40% of the time, and the listener other 60%. Making too much eye contact can make your partner uncomfortable, and too little eye contact can make the impression that you are disinterested.

During a social conversation the gaze of the participants will stay on the triangular region between the eyes and the lips. In business discussions the gaze will normally be directed at the triangular region between the eyes and forehead. However if the gaze stays away from the face, and persistently resides on the chest or pelvic region, it reveals the intention to seduce.

If direct eye contact makes you uncomfortable, imagine a triangular area between eyebrows and lips of the speaker and fix your gaze within the area. Don't draw your gaze below the face. And avoid looking away in the mid sentence. If you feel the urge to avert the gaze, don't do it hastily; remember that you have the choice to blink. Maintain normal blinking, otherwise your look will be intense and will make your partner uncomfortable.

Reading the Body Language

In order to decide whether you'll carry on the conversation with your partner, it is paramount to recognize the kinesics of acceptance and rejection. We all are familiar with the signs people use for affirmation, approval and negation. Say for example nodding is a universal gesture for affirmation and recognition, except for few countries like Bulgaria and Albania. When people nod in slow rhythm during a conversation, it reflects that they are analyzing and fully agreeing with your words; it also means that they are interested in what you have to say. If nodding is accompanied by warm smile, it means that a rapport is being created. When you nod, you are actually displaying your eagerness to hear from others and encouraging them to become more expressive.

However if the listener nods faster than usual, it shows that he has understood your point and wants you to switch to the next point. The faster the rate of nodding, the more impatient the listener is becoming. Along with rapid nodding, other signs of discomforts may also appear; like stretching the earlobe, or covering the ear with one hand. During a conversation, if you find someone reacting subconsciously like this, it will be wiser to change the topic or to pause, so that the recipient can express himself.

Shaking the head reveals that the subject is in the state of negation. If someone shakes her head slowly from one side to another, it may denote that although her primary mind-set is negative, she is still thinking it over. If the head shaking is unusually fast, it can indicate that the listener has already rejected your theories, declining further discussion and becoming impatient even angry. Vocalics or the study on features of voice, like tonality, pitch, volume and speed can also make us more informed about the subject's attitude.

Looking at the position of someone's feet, we can determine a person's level of interest towards ourselves. If the head of the subject is pointing towards you during a discussion, and the feet is pointing towards the other direction, it implies that she has lost interest in the conversation and intends to move away from you. If you observe patiently, you will also notice that her torso is also aligning with her feet, although the head is still directed towards you; and soon you will find yourself totally neglected when she finally moves away her head.

CHAPTER 4

Making The Talking Really Easy

In the previous chapters we have learned about the importance of oral communication and how to overcome the barriers of communication. We have also learned how to transform our body language to appear more friendly and inviting. Now we are ready to make real conversation.

Communication and speech expert Bill Lampton thinks that the first seven to seventeen seconds of a conversation is most crucial. You have to grab the attention of your counterpart within this time. If you are a master conversationalist, you won't feel any trouble walking into a room and start a conversation with someone within few seconds. But if you are not an expert, you may be thinking what you can possibly say in ten seconds that will make your target really interested to hear more from you. The truth is there are numerous ways to get someone's attention, to make someone enjoy speaking with you.

One of the easiest ways to get someone's attention is through a "ritual" question, what is popularly known as "icebreaker". This is quite an effective tool that you can use to initiate a conversation very easily. There are three types of ritual questions: question about an object, situational questions and question about a person.

Question About An Object

The method of asking question about an object involves noticing something the target is carrying, like a book, a dog, or a fashion accessory, then asking the question that requires the other person to give some information that relates the object. For instance, "What a wonderful dog! What's her name?" or "That's a nice wristband! Where did you get it from?"

You can ask questions simply about anything the person is carrying. Some items can give you a lot to talk about. Musical instruments for example are practically an invitation to ask questions about how long the person has been playing, what kind of music she likes to play and who her favorite artist is. The point is to make other person show interest in conversation, not to obtain information about the object.

Situational Questions

Situational questions depend on the situation you're in. It can be about weather, about sporting event, or food— you both have to be in the same situation. Here are some examples: "This is my first time at this event. How about you?" "What do you think about the theme choice for this event?" "What do you think of the music?" if you're at a restaurant and waiting in a queue with your target, you can ask questions like, "what do think of the food?" you may ask whether she has any recommendations.

You can combine situational question with 'object questions' if you're somewhere like a bookstore or a sports shop or a movie theater. Many great conversations had been initiated by asking what someone is reading.

There is another way to ask situational questions, which is by offering help to somebody who needs it. Before offering assistance, first mention as though she needs help... if she responds positively, go ahead. For example, you found one of your neighbors, who is a new tenant, unpacking her car and moving heavy suitcases. Now if you want to start a conversation, you could say, "Well, I happen to live in the same complex. It looks like you need some help. Would you like me to help you with unloading?". Then you can continue the conversation by asking questions like what brought her here, questions about her profession and so forth.

Always ask positive questions, or talk on the positive aspects of the topics, when you start your conversation with these ritual questions.

Question about the person

Asking something interesting about a person is also a great way to initiate a conversation. You can ask question about anything— nice hairstyle, beautiful tattoo, nice piece of clothing, even about that person's fitness. Sometimes people will give you a guarded response if they are not sure about why you're asking. But the moment they realize that you're admiring whatever it is you've noticed, they will be interested talking to you.

Here are some examples:

- "I love your hair. Who long did it take to get it done"

- "It's a beautiful dress! Where did you find them?"

- "What a wonderful tattoo! How did you find the artist/ how far did you have to travel to get that particular art?"

- "Nice tie! Where did you buy it?"

It will take you less than ten seconds to ask any of the above questions. These questions are open ended, which means you can't answer them by "yes" or "no" It is good to ask open ended situational questions to start a conversation, because asking open ended questions can encourage your counterpart to talk more. You can also ask close-ended questions, if you can follow them up with open-ended questions so that your counterpart can expand her previous answer a little.

Here are some sample open-ended questions:

- What is your very earliest memory as a kid?

- Why do you think some people don't like animals?

- How did you get your current job?

- How do you describe me to your friends?

- That's really awesome! What make you love it so much?

- Looking at your pictures, when have you been the cutest so far?

- How do you find the motivation to run so often?

- Why do you not like scary rides at an amusement park?

- What is the grossest thing you can think of?

Most people like open-ended questions because they enjoy sharing information about themselves. If you are not used to holding a conversation, you may feel as if you are intruding on someone by asking these types of questions; but this is not true.

However not everyone will like answering the ritual questions. If you ask someone a couple of open-ended questions, and he gives very short answers, it's an indication that he is not interested to continue the conversation. On the other hand if you ask someone a close-ended question and he gives you a long answer, you can be certain that person wants to talk to you.

When Someone Approaches You

Most of the advices included in this book are about walking up to people and initiating a conversation, assumes that no one will approach you in social event and start a conversation. But you have learned the basics, and if you apply your learning in social situations, one may take up on your non-verbal invitation and approach you. In this case, although you may smile while the other person approaching you, may feel a little nervous. How would you handle this situation?

If you are unused to talking to others, you may feel a bit tensed when someone approaches you to talk. As a result you may unconsciously change your posture— cross your arms on your chest and stop smiling. This can give a mixed message to the approaching person. The instigator may think that your mood has changed and perceive this as an insult.

Instead, open your arms and show the inviting gesture and allow your partner to get closer. Broaden your smile as she approaches— it is important to make her think that you are happy see her; and looking forward to talk to her. She will feel flattered knowing that you are giving her full attention.

Remembering Names

According to Dale Carnegie, "A person's name is to him or her the sweetest and most important sound in any language". You can say a person's name is the most important word to him. If we want to make friends quickly or easily get someone's attention we have to learn not to forget their names. But sometimes we get acquainted with someone new only to forget their names within seconds.

The good news is, there are methods we can apply to remember the names easily. First of all pay attention when people say their names. If the name is unfamiliar you can ask what it means. A common technique to remember a name is to link the person to a celebrity with the same name. With your mind's eye, scan the face of the person you are being introduced with. Look for any distinct feature. If the person is very handsome or beautiful, and you can't pick a feature, we can use a default feature; that is the nose. The next step is the hardest part where you will need a good amount of practice, which is turning the name into an image. First we have to look for a sound-alike or something that comes into mind when we pronounce the name. Say for example, we have to remember the name "Keith". We can use the word 'key' to associate with the name. You may argue that if we are remembering the person by remembering key, we may call this person Mr. Key instead of Mr. Keith; but that will not happen. You can also use sound-alike like 'teeth', if it comes in your mind. You can visualize this person with funny big teeth, like a clown. What about thief? Imagine the person is wearing a mask. It may sound ridiculous, but it does push that into a memory. Eventually all associations will fade and you will remember the name and the face.

Turning the Spotlight Around

Dominating the conversation may feel good, but we have to remember that conversation is more effective when both participants share information. It is important to turn the spotlight on your counterpart when you find that he is getting less opportunity to express his views. Sometimes you may need to turn the conversation to a topic about which he passionate to get him accept the spotlight.

CHAPTER 5

The Power of Small Talk

Most of us award small talk a low status. It's been trivialized and downplayed as surface-speak, a time waster usually by the people who are bad at it. But small talk is more important than many of us think. It's the core essence of how 99% of all relationships are formed.

Small talk starts with the first round of introductory questions and answers— it may start with a random topic of conversation such as weather in Santa Monica to a profound meaningful one such as global warming or how artificial intelligence will change the future. In most cases, it is with someone you just got acquainted with or have had very little previous interaction. It is how conversation begins when you are sitting next to someone on a train, on a plane or in waiting room. It may start with a simple question and answer, which continues until the point where it starts to deepen when one of the participants starts to reveal some personal information. The beauty of small talk is that it stimulates a wide range of electrifying emotions bringing a new level of understanding between people.

Small talk allows you and your counterpart to feel each other out, determining whether you're willing to continue the conversation.

Making Small Talk

Starter Kit

In today's world small talk is hard to avoid. Small talk is not an innate talent; you have to develop this skill with practice. The more you work your small-talk muscles, the stronger they become. Practice on the baker, the butcher and the candlestick maker. Ask about their skills. Talk to your co-workers. If you're working in a traditional office, where you see your co-workers everyday, you've lots of opportunities to interact with them. Ask simple questions like how their day is going so far. After your partner responds, continue with the conversation. Small-talk with your colleges while walking through the hallway, in the elevator, in the kitchen, in the cafeteria. Many times during the lunch break, you may find a group going to lunch at a local restaurant or café, one of the group members will ask you to join the group. Make sure to join the group for lunch during the first week on the job. It will give you the opportunity not just to boost your small talk skill but also to improve your working relationship with your colleagues. Here are some neutral topics for small talk with your co-workers:

- Today's weather

- Work

- Traffic or the daily commute (if you're living in a big city)

- Funny or unusual news

- Popular television programs, recent blockbuster movies

- Viral YouTube videos

- Sports or local sport events

- Weekend plans, holiday plans, vacation plans

- Complements on hairstyle, clothing.

- Foods, especially when it is breakfast or lunch time

Topics to avoid:

- Age

- Physical appearance

- Religion

- Politics

- Past relationships

- Anything PG-13 and up

Make a Habit

For some people small talk can be stressful and awkward. But small talk will become less intimidating if you know the rules of engagement and turn small-talk into a habit. Habit is mentioned because it is important in forming the person you are and the person you're becoming. By making a habit, you're changing the pattern of your mind, and training your mind into believing. Habits are generally created from our own experiences. When something feels good, we tend to keep doing it over and over, and that eventually turns into our habit. Habit can be good or bad— it can vary from smoking cigarettes to going to gym five days a week, to chatting with strangers on the subway as you commute to work.

Forming a habit usually takes 30 days. Therefore if you were to make small talk with the person next to you at your favorite coffee shop everyday for the next one month, it will turn into a good habit and your small-talk skill with significantly improve.

As you're chatting with different people everyday, your mind will subconsciously gather information and based on the responses of your counterparts, your mind will tell you what works and what doesn't. If the response is favorable, the mind will categorize this scenario as "things-that-work"; if the response is discouraging, the mind will toss this scenario into "things-that-don't-work" category. Based on your mind's feedback, you can either avoid the uncomfortable scenarios or figure out what went wrong, so that you can improve next time. Unless you learn experientially you'll never know what works what doesn't. With each social encounter, your mind and body will either reward you with a good feeling or a bad one.

The tone

According to Albert Mehrabian, successful communication is comprised of three parts— the words we use, our body language and the tone of voice. In a conversation, whatever the words we use, it's our tone that broadcasts what we're feeling when we say them. Sometimes when we say words we don't mean, our tone reveals our true intention. A person's tone of voice can either make or break in the first few seconds of small talk initiation. Therefore while engaging in small talks, pay attention to your voice and the way it sounds and adjust your voice so that how you say something has as much impact as what you say. Here are some tips for using your tone effectively:

Develop your ability to use a focused pause as you speak. If you too rapidly without many pauses, it can come across as nervousness. Your listener will also feel rushed, if you talk at a rapid pace. You may even find that the listener is struggling to catch what you are saying. Pausing gives the listeners time to absorb your words, and enables them to follow what comes next. It also helps you to feel comfortable in your words and how you express them. Pausing also allows you to take-in enough air to support your voice. Therefore if you talk very fast, make sure to punctuate with a pause.

While talking rapidly makes it hard to concentrate, talking too slowly can bore the listener. Therefore the ideal pace for speaking is not too slow and not too fast. Remember, the audiences are intrinsically lazy. If you don't make it easy for them, they won't put their effort into listening. The simple solution is to start at a moderate pace so that they can hear and understand your words, and not feel rushed or bored. If you are habitually a rapid speaker, here is an exercise for you by Marian Rich, a voice and speech teacher who coached many famous actors to improve their voice:

"Mark a paragraph / in this manner / into the shortest possible phrases. / First, / whisper it / with energetic lips, / breathing / at all the breath marks. / Then. / speak it / in the same way. / Do this / with a different paragraph / everyday. / Keep your hand / on your abdomen / to make sure / it moves out / when you breathe in / and moves in / when you speak."

Your habit of speaking too fast won't be cured overnight. Practice once a day for 21 straight days to see the result.

To reflect confidence in your voice, avoid speaking too softly or too loudly. Filler words such as, "Um", "ah", and "like" hinders your voice from flowing smoothly. Using filler words is not wrong, but using them too often can make you seem inarticulate and insecure. Filler words can easily get out of control if you're not conscious of them.

You don't have to completely avoid these words, but you should limit how frequently you use them, until you're comfortable with the persona you're projecting. Here is what you should do to shift your speech habits away from "um" and "ah" to more surefooted words:

- Notice how often you use those words. You may record yourself on audio or video, and ask a friend to find out if there's a word you repeat too much. Remember, in order to change something you've to acknowledge it.

- Make eye contact as you speak to people. If you make full, engaging eye contact with your counterpart while speaking, you'll feel uncomfortable to say, "Um".

- Organize your ideas before you deliver them. Chunk your sentences before you say them. Speak a short chunk of words, pause...then say another chunk. It will force you to slow down and help you to develop a rhythm.

- We often use filler words when our brain needs to catch up to our mouths. Slowing down a little can solve this problem. Talk a bit more slowly to reduce the gap.

- People who are afraid of creating an awkward silence, rush to fill the gap with filler words. But the lesser we're afraid of silence the quicker we can overcome it. Try to be silent when you're tempted to use those words. When you'll realize that silence is not bad, you won't bother using them.

- You may feel self-conscious, tensed, as you use filler words. Being self-conscious about how you're speaking will cause you to use more filler words. Ignore what other people might be thinking of you and relax.

Breath support or breath management is critical for free, relaxed speaking. Your breath support comes from your diaphragm, a dome shaped muscle located just beneath your lungs. Contraction of this muscle allows the air to enter into the lungs. Our diaphragm contracts as we breathe in and expands as we breathe out. Many of us don't fully engage the diaphragm, which causes reduced supply of oxygen into the lungs and as a result, we don't get enough breath support for speaking. Here is an exercise for increasing your awareness of breath support from the diagram.

- Lie on your back with your knees slightly bent

- Place your hands on your abdomen

- Now breathe normally and rest your attention on breathing from diagram. Be aware as your stomach rise and fall with in-breath and out-breath.

- Keep breathing and be aware of the inflow and outflow. Stay with your breath for five minutes.

- Now stand up. Repeat this exercise in the standing position.

Next time when you practice your speech, practice breathing and talking "from you belly button" feeling the pressure from the diaphragm.

Remaining confident is important when you meet someone and make a small talk. Nervousness tightens the throat constricting the airflow— and you'll feel that your breath is becoming rapid and shallow. Visualize yourself speaking confidently. For visualization practice, find a quiet place where you won't be disturbed for 5 minutes. Sit in a comfortable position with your back straight. Close your eyes and imagine yourself speaking confidently in front of a group of strangers. Feel relaxed and comfortable and breathe normally. Imagine the audience is eager to listen what you have to say. Imagine yourself as an eloquent speaker and pay attention to how you feel.

Beliefs sometimes turn into self-fulfilling prophecies. If you approach small talk with the belief that it will be dull and pointless, it probably will. Use positive affirmations described in chapter one to replace your negative beliefs with positive ones.

Active Listening

The common fear of making small talk with someone is that at some point of conversation, you will have nothing to say. Conversation is a back-and-forth process. So when someone finishes speaking, you have to say something back. But sometimes you have no idea what to say back, and it feels terrifying.

If you find yourself in a situation like this, there is a possibility that you're dealing with a fairly common conversational affliction— you were not paying attention what your counterpart was saying. Instead of paying attention on his words, you had focused all your attention on yourself, leaving you out of ideas when it was your turn to speak. People who are shy or introvert, frequently experience this problem. If this happen to you, don't be afraid. You can easily continue the conversation if you make a habit of listening attentively what your counterpart is saying. Active listening is critical for making small talk. When you're paying complete attention to the words of your counterpart, you are signaling that you are taking the speaker and his words seriously. This will encourage your partner to participate more in the conversation and a rapport will be created. Good body language also supports active listening. We've discussed it already. Lean forward, maintain the eye contact and nod to show you understand what your counterpart is saying. The other part of active listening is to understand what you're listening.

The Ripple Effect

If you throw a rock into water, it will produce a series of ripples spreading outward. Throw more rocks, the ripples will intersect with each other until they reach the edge of water. Conversation also follows the same rule— starting with the core topic picked by you or your partner, then switching to the next "ripple" or layer out, widening the scope of conversation. For instance you're starting the conversation about today's weather, then you expand the conversation to include topics like global warming.

Another example of using the ripple theory of conversation is when you meet someone at a restaurant. You can talk about the food, then expand outward to talk about other restaurants in this area. From there, you can talk about the business in this section of town, then town itself, and from there discuss the country. The amazing thing about the ripple theory of conversation is that you'll always have something to talk about— you'll never run out of ideas. Even if you feel that you've expanded the conversation as much as possible for one circle, you've the liberty to start a new circle that will intersect with the old circle. For instance if you expanded the conversation in the restaurant example to include your town, you can transition to another topic by discussing the city you both live, then asking your counterpart, what other cities he previously lived or would like to live. Once he replies, you can follow up with an open-ended question about city itself, and then expand from there.

Using the Information

While your counterpart speaking, listen actively, be aware about the personal information he gives to you. Based on the information he shares, you can discover the interests you have in common, then use them to expand the conversation. Be aware of the following types of information:

- Family and friends

- Hobbies

- Favorite sports

- Favorite music

- Favorite travel destination

- Favorite foods

- Favorite books

- Favorite movies

- Jobs

- Pets

- Vehicle

- Life goals

- Residence

- Political affiliation

The above items are just the samples of personal information that one can share about him or herself as the conversation progresses.

One of the common rituals of sharing personal information is asking what someone does for living. But if your counterpart is unemployed, or doesn't feel comfortable about taking about his current job, he or she may feel embarrassed to share this information. However there is a good way to ask this question without making your partner uncomfortable— ask him what your partner does with his time. This will give your partner the option to avoid revealing the information he feels uncomfortable about, and focus on the things he loves doing. Ask open-ended follow up questions if you want to learn more about him. Close-ended questions are also important to let your partner know that you're listening. But avoid asking too many close-ended questions in a row.

While discussing complex topics like politics or economics, you might want to sum up your counterpart's comments to show that you're listening. You can start summarizing by saying something along the lines of, "so what you're saying is..." or "So if I understand you correctly....". Once you're done, you can ask your partner if you've summarized correctly by saying, "is that right?". This allows your partner to either elaborate or correct your statement. Summarizing forces your mind to pay full attention to what the other person is saying and allows you sharpen your listening skill.

Exploring Common Interests

Although you're free to ask anything you like, the best questions are the ones your conversation partner feels passionate about. If you find a topic both of you feel passionate about, and discuss it, it will form an instant bond between you and your partner. You can spend much of a conversation talking about an interest that both of you share.

By finding an area of common interest, you can involve everyone into a conversation. Think about a successful conversation you had in the past with someone. Odds are that you were talking about something you both were passionate about. When you are discussing on a topic of common interest, you're not worrying about how to keep the conversation going or whether the other person is feeling bored. You can more easily talk about your passion than about the topics on which you don't have sufficient knowledge.

Once You Have the Information

After successfully continuing the conversation for a while, now you know what your counterpart does for living, his hobbies or may be the place where he lives. You might also be wondering, what to do with this information. The simple answer is, you can use them to learn more about him. Pick information that interests you, and discuss on this topic. Ask open-ended questions and a few close-ended questions.

Revealing Your Information

In chapter-one we have learned about self-disclosure. In this chapter we will discuss how to disclose personal information the right way. One of the ways to encourage your conversation partner to reveal their personal information is to disclose some of your own. Your partner already trusted you and revealed some of their personal information to you, now it is your turn to return the favor.

There are few methods to disclose personal information. The first rule is to start slowly. Decide whether you'll share your information after you're finished answering few introductory questions. These introductory questions are like verbal handshakes, which prepares the ground for self-disclosure.

Don't feel embarrassed if you find your information uninteresting comparing to that of your counterpart. For instance, you've just learned that your conversation partner is brokering a million-dollar business deal. You were about to tell him about your job— but now it does not seem worth mentioning. Don't feel intimidated to tell about yourself in a situation like this. Go ahead and say it anyway. Your counterpart may feel interested to know more about your job. If you feel positive about your work, you always have many good stories to share. Using your storytelling ability, you can make anything more interesting to listen.

Avoid exaggerating. While talking about yourself, you may skip the boring and routine parts of your life. But to sound exiting, you should not exaggerate. None of us are perfect— don't make yourself out to be perfect. Don't talk about a skill you don't have, don't say you've done something you have not; because if your partner eventually knows the truth, they will no longer trust you. You will lose their respect, which will be quite difficult to earn back.

Once your conversation partner has gained your trust, you'll want to tell more about yourself. Self-disclosure has different levels and they form a pyramid. Our habitual answers to people's questions are the bottom level of self-disclosure. These are, "all rights", "Oks" and "fines". People will know a very little about you when you'll use these answers. These answers indicate that you're in a positive mood and the other person is allowed to come up and talk to you. Once you're done answering the routine questions, you'll enter into the second level of the pyramid, which is revealing some factual information. Revealing the facts is safer than revealing feelings and emotions. Facts allow your partner to understand the real you. When all the members of the conversation disclose some facts and gain some understanding about their conversation partners, they can make a decision on whether they would take the conversation to the next level. Revealing facts is also safer than giving opinions, because when you're revealing your opinion you're giving people the choice of disagreeing with it. Giving opinion is the 3rd level of self-disclosure pyramid. The top level of the pyramid is your personal feelings. You'll only reveal your feelings to people who are very close to you, people who are important in your life. When you talk about your emotions, your hopes— you're making yourself vulnerable. Therefore you have to be careful before entering into the final level of self-disclosure. The good thing about revealing your feeling is that it will allow people know the person you really are, which will create a deeper bond between you and the person you're sharing information with.

Conversation and lecture are not the same. During conversation every participant actively join in the discussion. So if you talk for too long, the other person may eventually lose interest in the discussion. Therefore before going into too much detail, give your counterpart an opportunity to react. You may ask your counterpart questions on the topic of discussion to make sure the flow of information is balanced. Check if your partner is displaying the signs of active listening. If they seem bored and their attention is focused elsewhere, if they lean back, they are not probably paying attention to what you are saying. In this case you may want to shift the spotlight and allow the other person to talk.

Changing the Subject Gracefully

While you can spend a good amount of time talking about a common interest, you may want to change the topic at some point. The easiest way to change the subject of discussion is to remember the information your partner shared with you. Then when it is time to change the subject, simply say, "by the way, you were previously talking about..." then continue from there. This is a very effective technique because you're shifting the focus on your partner, allowing him to speak something that interests him. Your partner will appreciate this opportunity and feel encouraged to speak on the new topic. You can apply the same technique, if you want to revisit a previously discussed subject.

We already know that if ripple theory is applied in conversation, the participants never run out of ideas, as they always have something to talk about. While switching from one topic to another is not difficult, once you've transitioned to a new topic, spend few minutes on this topic before you switch to the next one. Frequently changing the topic of discussion gives your partner the impression that you don't particularly care about any of the topics being discussed or that you are not actively participating in the discussion. If their assumptions are right, you should calm down, think about a topic you both will enjoy, and steer the conversation to that topic.

If your partner is not interested to discuss your chosen topic, she may not tell you directly, but you can know it by noticing her responses: She won't ask you any follow up questions, and will give short, clipped answers to your questions. You will also find that she is reluctant to give you any free information on the topic. Defensive body languages like, crossing arms are also an indication that she is not enjoying this topic. If this is the case, you have to change the topic.

Avoiding a Topic

If you want to avoid a topic your partner wants you to discuss, you can politely tell him, "I would prefer not to talk about that. Let's talk about something else". Or you can say, "Why don't we talk about something more interesting?" Then pick a subject you both are interested in.

CHAPTER 6

Exiting a Conversation

Imagine you are at a social event, and you're stuck in a conversation with someone you just met. Common courtesy dictates that you don't cut someone off mid-conversation, but you want navigate the room and meet other people. What will you do?

Although exiting a conversation can sometimes be more difficult than starting one, the good news is there are several ways to leave a conversation gracefully. Many of us don't know how to smoothly leave a conversation— that's why most conversations end awkwardly. But we want to leave a warm impression— make everyone involved feeling fulfilled about the conversation so that they want to speak to us again.

Many people don't know the right time to exit a conversation— they wait too long trying to bow out. Experts think that the right time to end a conversation is when you're done exchanging your views or when you feel that the time is right to end the conversation. But sometimes it is hard to know if you have finished exchanging your views. According to experts, knowing when you're done communicating your points is quite easy; but individuals who are not expert conversationalists fail to identify this point because they put their attention on other aspects of conversation. If you have a little experience in interpersonal communication, you may pay most of your attention on actively listening and understanding other's views and presenting your views. Being able to step back and see if you've reached the point takes some degree of practice.

In the middle of the conversation, while your counterpart is talking, spend a couple of seconds to ask yourself what you want to say next. We all do it probably without thinking about it. But this time you're doing it consciously. If you find that you've reached a point where you have nothing to add into the conversation, then it is time to leave the conversation.

Knowing how to end the conversation is relatively easier than knowing when to end the conversation. There are four steps to leave a conversation gracefully. The first step is to reiterate your counterpart's idea. By doing this you are signaling your partner that you no longer want to carry on this conversation. You're also assuring your partner that you're paying full attention to his ideas. The next step is a vital part of exiting a conversation. In this stage you'll tell your partner that you've enjoyed talking to him. You should not sound apologetic. While it is the best way to end the conversation, it can be uncomfortable for some people. If it was good conversation, you may feel the urge to explain why you are leaving. Here are some possible reasons to excuse yourself from a conversation:

- I need another drink

- I'm going to make a quick restroom trip

- I want to make sure to say hello to everyone here

- I have to get back to work

It is better not to lie, when you're giving an excuse to leave the conversation; because it may damage your credibility. The final part is saying goodbye to your conversation partner.

Although the four-step conversation leaving technique is one of the best ways for exiting a conversation, it is not the only way. There are many other ways. Here are two of them:

Invite another person into the conversation. Introduce them to each other. Then quickly excuse yourself. This is a very easy way to leave a conversation, but the downside is that you're not dealing with the issue, you're only passing it off to someone else.

Faking a cellphone call is another good technique to quickly exit a conversation. Fake a cellphone call in the middle of the conversation; then pretend to answer the phone and walk away. The problem with this technique is that it is based on lying. If your partner is watchful enough to notice that your phone neither played a ringtone, nor vibrated, it will hurt his feeling. This can negatively affect your reputation especially in a business convention.

There is another problem with faking a cell phone call, which is your partner might decide to wait until you're done with the phone call.

CONCLUSION

Now you are equipped with many powerful tools that you can use to talk to anyone, anywhere and anytime with confidence. You know how to overcome the major communication barriers and how to use your body language for effective communication. You also know how to initiate small talk, how to keep the conversation going and how to successfully exit a conversation. But knowing the methods is not enough; you have to practice them regularly and gain mastery. Being a master communicator takes lots of practice. Stick to your practice and in time when you'll gain expertise, you'll be surprised to see how powerful conversation skill can transform your life in a positive way.